Somewhere in My Heart

Somewhere in My Heart

A Passionate Florilegia

PRACHI BEHRANI

PARTRIDGE

A Penguin Random House Company

To order additional copies of this book, contact
Partridge India
000 800 10062 62
orders.india@partridgepublishing.com

www.partridgepublishing.com/india

Contents

To HIM, Mom, Dad and the Joy of writing

To all of you, who have inspired me and would
continue to inspire me in the future

And, most importantly to her without whom this couldn't have been possible

Oh, Yeah. Also to him who'd kill me if I don't put
his name here. My brother, Rishabh

The Rhyme

When the world is occupied
And one needs to while some time
In the worlds of fantasies to hide,
Shelters, one, under the blankets of sweet, sweet rhyme.

The rhyme that stays
In the hearts of all,
Like the sun rays,
When the winters fall.

The rhyme that is,
The cure for the oppressed
Like the mother's kiss
On the stranded forehead.

The rhyme that ails,
To all the wrong.
Through the heart it sails,
Like the melody of a song.

The rhyme blooming,
Like the sweetest of flowers.
To all the pain soothing
Even at the unearthly hours.

The rhyme that cures
To the heart that bleeds.
Like the dew that lures
And to the morning leads...

The rhyme that pervades,
In each and every heart.
Forever it stays,
And never does it part.

What Makes Me Write

I could not weave a story
When laughter filled my heart
But I can write an endless tale
Since my soul is torn apart.

I could not compose
When joy had place
Now i can write a prose
When woes I turn to face

I had blurred sight
With life so perfect
I hold myself tight
Now that reality I reflect.

Because life is filled with ups and downs
Bits of smiles and many a frowns...

Society

I worked really hard
they called me a nerd.
I stopped working and relaxed
they said I didn't care.
I walked to work
they said I was poor.
I drove till there
they called me a brat.
I wore a jeans
they said I was too conservative.
I wore shorts
They said I was exposing much.
I had no friends
they said I was naive.
And when I did
they said I faked love.
I was happy
They said that they loved my presence.
I was upset for once
They said that they hated my company.

Once they stopped talking to me
they started talking about me.
Because they never stop talking.
They never stop thinking.
I decided not to listen to them.
Not to change my views for them.
If I ever took a decision
I decided not to change it, for them.
And they stopped saying, one day.
And started accepting
What I was.

Love

Love isn't about,
Forgiving each other.
Its about having no doubt,
That your beloved,
Can ever be wrong.

Love isn't possessive,
To hold on to the other.
Its rather submissive,
To let do as we want,
To the one you love.

It isn't about imposing,
Restrictions for their safety.
Rather about raising,
Them enough to be able,
On their own to be safe.

Love says not always,
Words as sweet as sugar.
It scolds on certain days,
Because "to err is human"
And requires heat to grow.

Love isn't about not letting,
The other one go.
Its about free, them setting,
And waiting while they return,
To see what they've achieved.

Love isn't about those precious gifts,
Nor is about the pampering we receive.
Rather about pushes and the lifts,
From our beloveds,
That to success led.

Love doesn't ever forget,
The gestures of love shown.
It doesn't ever fret,
If it doesn't get,
What it expects.

Love is always kind,
And ready to forget.
It doesn't ever mind,
Little mistakes,
That happen all the time.

Love receives all the pain,
And the joys if to give.
Like the joyous rain,
that bathes the soil,
And dirt does eat.

Love doesn't demand,
Nor does it complain.
It doesn't reprimand,
To the lover's nature,
But accepts as they are.

Love is as pure,
As the springs of dove.
All woes does it cure,
Of, the one ones who love...

Mum and Dad

You told me what is wrong,
And what all is right.
And sang the lullaby song,
When I was up all night.

You acted mad,
Just to make me smile.
Thank you Mum and Dad,
For being there all this while.

Helping me with studies,
And scolding me at times.
Helping me make buddies,
And teaching me those rhymes.

Waking me up for school
And tucking me in the bed with a story.
Racing with me in the pool,
And letting me win with glory.

Letting me grow
But being at my side.
Happiness or woe,
Nothing could I hide.

Facing my youth,
For you may not be an easy task.
But you accept it like the truth,
No questions do you ask.

More than my peers,
And more than the Lord up there,
Since all those years,
For me do you care.

For this unconditional love,
Do I thank you.
Look at the sky above
That's how much I love you.

Battlefield

During the sojourn of life,
One will always witness,
Through thorns we have to thrive,
And the love for roses, harness.

Storms have a peace,
That the peaceful winds do not.
The battlefields would please,
More that the luxuries bought.

The ones who fight,
Are the ones who win.
The others to their plight,
Their own lives ruin.

You

You mean what to me,
Can't be said or be told.
Oh, can't you see
You, I forever wish to hold.

The soothing sunshine,
to my wintry life.
The diamond's mine,
To a flaunty wife.

You are the drop of rain
In the scorching heat
And to all the pain
Relief do you meet.

The three wishes of magic,
In the lamp of wonders.
And a shelter's hug in the tragic,
When cry the thunders.

You are the cover,
When worries loom over.
And the lover,
When times are lower.

You are the rainbow,
That colors forever.
Of the sight that doesn't let go,
And fades never.

You are the fifty shades,
Of the color grey .
And the aids,
When the troubles lay.

In the velvety sky,
The stars that shine.
Though you be so high
Baby, you are mine.

She was the Juliet, and he, her Romeo

Dwelt among the trodden ways
Besides the spring of dove
Butterflies did she chase
Seeking for her love

With hues of genius on his cheek
In the finest tones could he speak
While he was just a boy
For all had he been the dearest joy!

She was all
He could think about
For her did he fall
Love in his heart did sprout

Truly he loved her
And was she unaware
Softer than the fur
Her fair skin did he stare

As it was night
He climbed up her balcony
Gathered up all his might
Just because he loved his honey

Her eyes as twilight fair
Shitter shatter did she blink
Like twilight too her dusky hair
And her lips strawberry pink.

She thought of him as a phantom of delight
And did she blush at his every sight
He in her heart she kept
Looking at him, her had leapt

They finally met!
Finished was all the woe!
She was the Juliet,
And he, her Romeo

When were they along
Forgotten was all the pain
Nature sang a jolly song
And elated was the rain!

But then,
Their families wanted them apart
Without each other to be.
Broken was her heart
Frustrated was he.

Couldn't they anything say
Or do anything about
Silent on the ground she lay
Inside her heart, did she shout.

He thought she was no more
Changed to him every horizon
His heart ached till the core
And that's when he sipped the deadly poison

Up she woke,
When saw the mud bed
Her heart there broke
Because he was dead

Under her feet
Did he lie
Her luck she couldn't beat
He really did die

Her life was a waste
In the bloody valley dooms her heart had sank
and then in haste
A sip of poison she drank

She never cried
Even after all the woe
Instead she died
To meet her Romeo

They had finally met
In the Good Heaven's love row
She was the Juliet
And he, her Romeo!!!

All I Have

Not the health
That makes immune.
Not the wealth
That's the greatest boon.

Not the looks
That catch attention
Not the books
That deserve the greatest mention.

Nor were these,
At all mine.
But with ease
I carried them fine.

Claiming to own
Mine that never really was
Wish I had known
What inspires with awes

Mine was the Rhyme
The prose I told
My poetry was sublime
Me, forever did it hold.

Promise You wont Leave

They've all been doing it ever since,
Never staying forever.
Too thrash my heart like mince,
They've been so clever.

Goodbyes aren't so good,
I'll be backs not so true,
Roaming alone in the woods,
Bubbles of fantasy I drew.

Someday they'll all be back
Just on the right track.
Right besides me,
Oh! You'll see...

But if not, if so not
My blood would clot, My heart would heave.
And BECAUSE you matter the most,
promise that you won't ever leave

Where Rainbows End

When rises from the east, the sun,
To the darkness or autumnal slumber shun.
Kicking off the morning the spring springs,
With blossom and the life takes the wings.

And that's when I met you,
Forgetting all my pain.
Strong were the winds that blew,
Elated was the rain.

But the we had to go,
Our ways apart.
My heart felt low,
Like struck by a dart.

My heart, I had to mend,
We had to part,
And that's where the rainbows end.

Why is it always a Girl

Why is it always a girl
Who is killed in the womb
Why abuses does the world hurl
To her, who builds her own tomb .

Why is she
Not given enough care
Why does every man be
Out for her skin bare

Why is she seen
As a toy for the bed
Why has she always been
With shame filthily red.

She isn't given a chance to speak
Or express her heart out
Considered to be meek
Just supposed to pose and pout.

The man ungrateful
Mars his own creator
He turns hateful
To his only mentor.

For every women
The same old tale
Responsible are the men
For her life so stale

She carries tears
In her eyes
And terrorized fears
To her demise

Would this never end
Is she meant to be a slave
For the men who send
From her bed to her grave.

Flaws

Like doesn't blow
Without the holes the flutes.
The world doesn't do
Without the disputes.
The moon has spots
Yellow leaves in lush green trees
Even the reddest of apple rots
Holes to be seen in cheese.

Flaws make life
What it is meant to be
Yet we thrive
To correct whatever we see.
Imperfections add beauty
To the essence of the soul.
It isn't our duty
Rather the God's role.

Loneliness

The Pathos of a man's isolation
Can be felt solo by him
And not by the entire creation
Can be understood
The eyes that brim.

Pain, the hearts bears
Times are bleak
Woefully trickle down the tears
Moist is the cheek

To one, people are hardly bound
No one seems to care
Though can be heard many a sound
But of own, seem rare.

Heartbeats are stopped
Each breath is a mess
The heart itself is lopped
Eternal is the LONELINESS

Alone

I dwelt alone as a lonely cloud
Terribly away from the filthy crowd.
If joyous or if woeful they be
They had enough of company,
To pour their hearts out
And share everything about.
Whether I lived or if I died
If I rejoiced or if I cried
I had just the company
Of no one else but only me.
To perpetually cry out
To scream and needily shout.

I closed my eyes
Reducing the world to subzero size.
Longer longing along the time
The Almighty blessed with my soul's rhyme.
He looked within my soul
And filled the empty dreadful hole.
No longer did I have to moan.
No longer ALONE did I feel ALONE.

Teacher

When God was kind
And wanted a helping creature
That would heal many a mind
He created a teacher.

And that's when I met you
Forgetting all my pain
Strong were the winds that blew
Elated was the rain

You're the life
A good mother, teacher, and wife
You're the best
Much better that the rest

You know my low points
And the problems I face
You're my bone joints
If my life is a race

Hope you always stay blessed
and keep blessing those
Whose life is almost messed
With your heart as fragrant as rose

Without you
I can't even imagine to be
I truly respect you
For all you cared for me.

A person like you
I couldn't have ever met
Such a mentor are you
I'm lucky to get.

You'd always be there
In the piece of my heart
You provided me with ultimate care
Of my life, the most important part.

You're my teacher
a second mother to me
I'm your preacher
Loyal, to you I'd always be.

Daddy's Princess

It started when I was born
Never became less
Everyone knew what was going on
I was my daddy's princess

Then i was seven
Te bought me a pink dress
It felt like heaven
Because I was my daddy's princess

And then I was sixteen
My life was a mess
So close had he been
Because I was my daddy's princess

I had to get married
He became so restless
Me, in his arms he carried
As to him, I was the one and only princess

I had a child
God, was that wild!
But he couldn't care less
Because I was my daddy's princess

He couldn't care stay more
Leaving me all alone
My heart ached till the core
I couldn't help but mourn

No matter what
My life has brought
M wouldn't love him less ever
I'll stay my daddy's princess forever!!!

As I remember the days
When I was treated like a princess
To me he did everything to faze
To cheer me up, were his ideas of maze.

I got everything I always wanted
Living a dream
To my friends I had always flaunted
Royal...did it seem

I'm a lucky girl
Whose dreams came true
Was treated like a pearl
Like a bird I flew

But then thunderstruck
Against me, was my luck
My father- he had left
And my heart, it was theft.

Even though he's no more
My heart, still so sore
yet,
I wouldn't love him less ever,
Id stay my daddy's princess forever!!!

Dear Mum

As the sun rises,
So do my tears.
I see my pillow,
Moist wist with tears.

As I cry in the shower every day,
Missing the nights when you lay,
Close to my heart, my soul!!!

I fear of the days still to come,
Oh dear mum..! Oh dear mum!
Nights are dark, not a great lark,
i miss you more, from my heart's core!

Oh dear mum,
Wish you knew,
What was going on,
It was you and only you,
Since I was born.

It isn't easy for me,
Without you to be!!!
Worries are more, happiness some,
Oh! dear mum, Oh, dear mum!

Her Dusky Hair

Her dusky hair fell
At dawn, on her rosy cheek.
Her deep eyes did tell
That the times were bleak.

To give her some joy
Came a manly, young boy.
Who was a gift,
By creations to make her spirits lift.

She looked like she had got all.
In love did she fall.
And he loved her too,
In love, were the birds, two.

Her eyes, shutter shatter did blink
And they said what
Her lips strawberry pink
Ever could say not.

She looked down
Shy in a timid style.
The glow of the entire town
As if hid in her smile.

She tried to hide her blush,
With the curtain of her hair.
But in a rush,
Blew it the air.

Even the winds did wish
With all their heart.
To see them flourish,
And never, ever to part.

Love and Pain

As calm as dove,
And as ferocious as rain.
Are the feelings of love,
And woefully heartbreaking pain.

The pain scoops out,
The pieces of heart.
Even if you scream and shout,
Your soul still breaks apart.

It springs with joy too,
And the moments are magical.
The worlds I LOVE YOU
Forever are to stay sensational.

Best Friends Forever

To you I turn when my spirits need a lift
To you I treasure Because our friendship is a gift
To you I look up when I'm in pain
For you to make up my mood with your talks insane

Your smile lights up the entire day
My life blossoms with the words you say
You were there the nights I wept
Looking at you my heart had leapt

When was everyone gone
And I bewildered all alone
Only you didn't leave me
With me, you promised ever to be

My heart truly says
We would stay together always
Wouldn't ever let you down
Wouldn't ever smile if you frown

We share the laughs, we share the tears
We share the jokes and all the fears
We might be quiet to everyone else
But to the other, everything, each one tells

Would part never
Would stay best friends forever
Your presence brings me joy
That's what we are, a BFF girl and a BFF boy!

Boy, I Missed You

You weren't there
Hardly anyone to talk to
Cried till my heart went bare
Boy I missed you

Was the world around
But I didn't care
To you I was bound
But you weren't there

Wish I could clutch
You next to me
I missed you so much
Together, we were made to be

I faked a smile
Woes inside me did pile
I tried to have fun
Though, I could have none.

Offered much aid
people who were new
But for you I was made
Just wanted to be with you!

Wanted you to be there,
Someone to talk to
Someone for me to care
Boy I missed you!!!

Bitch

Twinkle twinkle little snitch
Mind your business nosey BITCH
Sweet at face and sour at back
Human behavior do you lack.

When you walk the earth shivers
Looking at you the world quivers
Well I hate you and you hate me
More worse than this you couldn't be.

So here I write you a prose.
Even though you're hell gross.

Children of God

When we are snug close and worm to Mum and Dad,
They still pray for a parent to tell What's good and What bad.
We get bikes and cars and gifts and blessings on birthdays,
They don't have a single person to mourn even on their death days.

After dinner we go to bed,
They still pray for some piece of bread.

Although tears of helplessness flowed into their eyes,
Woefully starved were their cries,
We still pass by ,
leaving them alone to cry.

We've got a home, a family ane life's every bit,
What they have? Forget it!
Still we cry,
What a sigh!

Let's pray for their future,
For a life free of such torture.
God, help them please,
A sweet life with a little ease.

Propose

He looked into my eye
And went on his knee
I could see him cry
Wanting me, his to be

I LOVE YOU he mumbled,
His voice so meek
His hands trembled
As he touched my cheek.

Said it was true love, did he
Said even a moment away from me did seem long
Wanting me his to be,
He sang a sweet song.

He called me his princess
His Angel, sweetheart and mistress
Said without me his life would wither,
Said, the both of us were meant to be together.

He brought in front the bouquet of rose
And the teddy he had hid behind his back
Impressive was his way of propose
Not even a bit did it lack.

Valentine

The flowers would blossom,
The sun would shine.
I'll be thy bosom,
And be wholly thine.

The night would chitter,
And the cat would twine.
The stars would glitter,
And you'll be mine.

Would there be not a pain,
And no one would whine.
Magical would be the holy rain,
And love would make as high as wine.

To make love more divine,
Would thou be my valentine?

Even If...

Even when waters leave the ocean,
The birds leave the sky.
The heat leaves the sun.
Won't Angel leave her Joy.

Even when shivers leave the cold,
And the droplets leave the rain.
The glitter leaves the gold,
And tears leave the pain.

Even if the breaths left are few,
I won't leave ever you.

Mistake

Everybody makes mistakes,
I made one too.
Oh! My heart breaks,
As nothing about it can I do.
Why did you leave me?
And go so far apart.
Oh!Why can't you see,
It also breaks my heart.

Risen up has the guilt,
Inside me which had built.
Forgive me please,
I aint.at all, at ease.
Because I know I have caused pain,
But I promise...I won't do it again.

"More hurt, than the one who is hurt,
is the one, who hurts."

Not one of those

I wouldnt ever be, just another girl,
Who ends up leaving.
First treats you like a pearl,
And then leaves you grieving.

I wouldn't just, use you and then throw,
First love, and then suddenly go.
I wouldn't ever leave
And in you, I'd forever believe.

Love you till eternity will I,
With your tears I shall cry.
Being in your arms, be my only choice,
And in your joy I shall rejoice.

I won't ever be one of those.
With no fragrance a counterfeit rose.

Now Does My Heart Heave

Now does my heart heave,
Because I had promised that I won't leave.
I had no choice so,
Away did I have to go.

I miss you so much
Do I miss your voice's touch.
To no one can I my heart pour.
Even though it is still so sore.

I can't even ask you to return
Even though to you I still am smitten.
My heart it's essence does lack,
Because I know that I cant have you back.

Of you I was so fond,
So close was our soul's bond.
The hollow of my heart you could fill,
But only if you could forgive me still.

Euthanasia

I've seen him live his death,
He dies by inches you bet.
Right to live, Right to die
Let it go by, make a try.
Euthanasia, some word it seems,
Deadly life's ugly beams.
Every breath trapped in the throat,
Let it escape, in God's sweet coat
Don't let live, Don't let die
Why even bother to try?
Every moment of his life
Is like a walk on a silly knife.
Let him live, Let him die
Let him make a little try...

Freedom

Freedom is the rain drop,
Falling free on the hill.
And the dew on the tree top,
In the morning of chill.

It is the bird that sings,
To wake the world from slumber.
Its the bee that stings,
At times, the biggest blunder.

It's the cloud wandering,
high up in the sky.
And the bird's wing,
She flutters to fly.

It is the child that runs,
Behind the kite that flies.
The event that stuns,
And makes you wise.

It is being in charge of your time,
And not going by the watch.
It is the joy to sublime,
While the sunset you watch.

It is dancing in the rain,
And having no one to judge.
Like having a chance for the tears to drain,
And having no one to nudge .

It's like laughing out loud,
Without any fears.
Of the self being proud,
And hugging like bears.

It is the rope.
One can either put to use.
Or by hanging the self,
gravely misuse.

Fun

Fun isn't just watching your favorite cartoon,
Nor is it playing the game you love.
It isn't just staring at the glittering moon,
On the starry sky above.

It isn't about gossiping endless,
With your beloved friends.
It isn't about creating a mess,
Careless about making amends.

It isn't just playing football,
Nor is it playing drums.
It isn't going to the mall,
Or throwing tantrums.

It isn't dancing to the beat,
Nor is it partying crazy.
It isn't playing in the heat,
Till the vision goes hazy.

It isn't reading your favorite novel,
In the comfort of your own bed.
It isn't decorating the canvas,
With splashes of blue and green and red.

It isn't experimenting carelessly,
Nor making sculptures of clay.
It isn't singing tunelessly,
Nor enacting your favorite play.

It isn't just enjoying a ton,
No it isn't any of these.
What actually is fun,
Is rather all of these.

I Still Think of You at Times

I still think of you at times,
And those days gone by.
Can't fit in my rhymes,
Those days, even if I try.

You changed me,
And my life so much.
Without you I couldn't be,
My soul did you touch.

Used to talk day and night,
And still couldn't get enough.
Loved with all our might,
And still ended up SO ROUGH.

Abuses did you hurl,
And said the words that killed.
Crying all nights, my soul did curl,
And with tears, my pillow filled.

Got back together soon,
Better than the way it used to be.
Felt like being on the moon,
And even the entire world could see.

But that didn't last forever too,
Maybe we weren't meant to be.
Nothing we bothered to do,
Wanted to part did we.

Was it a relief,
And did it seem free.
Like a fresh green leaf,
Fallen off a tree.

None did none lack,
Or even thought about.
Didn't we need each other back,
There was no doubt.

But now as I sit and think,
Of the days as colourful as a rainbow.
My heart does sink,
Because you were good a friend, and worse a foe.

I'll Miss You

I miss the things we did
The kisses we blew
The secrets we hid
And the way you said "I Love You"

I miss every word you said
The way you stared
The kiss on my forehead
The way you cared

Miss the ring you wore me
And the way we hugged
We knew we were meant to be
So, close together we tugged.

Miss how your hand had felt
Firm, on my waist
The way did I melt
And hugged you in haste.

My arms around your neck
Yours lovingly holding me
The way you planted a peck
Love in your eyes could I see.

Miss the touch on my cheek
Miss the first kiss
Now that times are bleak
Everything do I miss.

We'll be together
And this time forever
To believe this, we have to.
Till then, you miss me...
And... I'LL MISS YOU.!

Socrates

By Socrates the great were questioned
All the issues in the world that were mentioned
Who, What, Where and Why
To everything did he sigh.

To ask is to confirm
Did he have a strong belief
His views were firm
Giving him a blossoming relief.

He questioned almost everything
Not leaving a bit
List of intelligent questions did he sing
To the issues that sensibly couldn't fit .

His students and the ones he mated
Only seemed to admire
Rest everyone hated
His habit to inquire.

Series of questions did he brim
Inquired the entire world
People started to hate him
Death to him the judges hurled.

Socrates the great
The father of philosophy
Met a fearful end
For his inquiring strategy.

But he gained respect
And taught to ask
Life's every prospect
Did he unmask.

First Love

I've always heard
First love mostly never fails
Was it just a cliche or word
Realized have I, away it trails

The initial of it is wobbling fun
Sparkling magic and many a turn
Soothing around is the breeze
Elated exceptionally is mind's unease

The person might not even know
Yet the feeling is firm
Love isn't a woe
Of the heart the sweetest germ

It might sound fun
Or cause you to smile
Away from it can't one run
Happiness inside does come alive.

The one you truly love,
Might not even love you back
With helplessness in the springs of dove
Your life do you track

The heart in pieces does break
To the core does it ache
To be in love, is to be lost
Facing the woes is to pay the cost.

Unlike I heard,
My first love did seem to fail
Love is a free bird
Comes on it's own,
Own it's own away it trails.

The Teacher would Rather

One screams,
And jokes the other make.
One dreams,
Even while he is awake.

One cannot respect,
And the other is always in a haste.
One, although, intellect,
His time does he waste.

One is always late,
And the other is always cursing.
And so he doesn't have a single mate.
And maybe requires a serious nursing.

The teacher would rather,
Leave than teach the mess.
That's all we gather,
From what she says.

Water Cycle

When rises from the east the sun
To the darkness or autumnal slumber shun
Kicking off the morning the spring springs
With blossom and life takes the wings

And that's when the sun did his act
Giving the evaporation impact
Formed were water vapors by the cooling sensation
And that's why we call it condensation.

Long were the trees that grew
Shining was the window pane
Strong were the winds that blew
Elated was the rain

No one felt low
Pretty was the rainbow
Round, around traveled a single particle
In a nutshell is bound, our water cycle

What Made Me Cry

I remember it
From the beginning to the end
How my life you lit
Till the day bent.

How I smiled
When I saw you at first
Bubbles of fantasy I piled
Not thinking about the rest

Going to the store
And to the park
Enjoying till the core
Till it was dark

Doing the lame act
That crazy kind
And leaving the silly impact
In the piece of your mind

You helped me past the dog
An act that would always tweet
Or in my thoughts would it jog
Because it was just so sweet

You missed the football match
Just to be with me
You took away a patch
Part of my heart that had to be.

Waiting for someone
Just to get a picture clicked
When we found no one
It was the maid we picked

Giving the secret blush
And the lunch we ate
Sharing the strawberry crush
Before quarter to eight

As the clock struck eight, you had to go
I wanted to leave, you till there
My heart felt low
My skin felt bare.

Wasn't easy to let you go.
Or to say bye
It was such a mo
And that's what made me cry.

Happy Birthday

Happy Birthday to you,
My dear sweetheart.
May God bless you
And may we never part.

It's your special day,
May you rejoice
Wish whatever you may
And get all the joys

May you glow
And may you shine.
May the world know
That you'd always be fine.

And on this special day
For you I would pray.
And all I'd like to say,
Is Happy Birthday

It's just so Wow

You are my mum's age
Your kids are that of mine
Still are friendship we stage
Understand the each other oh-so-fine!

We hangout together
And have wobbling fun
Laugh feeling as light as a feather
With sparkling magic and many a turn.

Your smile lightens up my entire day
My life blossoms with the words you say
We promise to part never
And stay best friends forever.

I remember when I first met you
A friend did I gain
Strong were the winds that blew
Elated was the rain.

We came closer
And knew each other well
Never were we posers
To each other, everything, did we tell

And we were so close then
And so are we now
It felt like heaven
And now... It's just so WOW.....!

Teenage is an Iconoclasm

At the age of confusion,
Our lives seem an illusion.
Experiencing ennui every day,
Is it fine to experience envy, what say?

Facebook seems better than the other books,
What we care about is just our looks.
Want to get popular,
Friends seem spectacular.

Want wings to fly,
Such silly reasons to laugh and cry.
This guy seems better that that ,
Day by day, I'm growing fatter than fat.

OMG! What am I supposed to do?
Face the problems or hide in the loo.
Wish I were like her.
My vision is nothing but a world which is blur.

Want to get a good score,
Yet studies seem bore.
Somebody please help me
Look at the world the way I see.

Little Brother

He'll drive you crazy
He'll irritate you
At times he'd be so lazy
In his own world with many a mew.

He'd make you smile
He'd make you frown
Himself around he'd jiggle
Sweetly insane like a clown.

Cuter than the cutest
Is his smile
Bruter than the brutest
Is his rile.

The best gift from my mother
Is special, my Little Brother.

Jealous Guy

You are insecure,
And that's what makes you cry.
You think I might not love you anymore,
You are just a jealous guy.

Keeping me away,
From those boys you try.
All my friends say,
You're just a jealous guy.

On all my little acts
Do you keep an eye,.
You're not at all lax,
But, just a jealous guy.

If my phone is busy,
A million times do you try.
You make me dizzy,
You're just a jealous guy.

You get mad at me,
And at times I don't even know why.
Why do you have to be
Such a jealous guy.?

Yet, It has made me smile,
And it has made me cry.
Because all this while,
You've been a jealous guy.

It gives me pleasure,
Like the only star in the sky.
To you, I treasure,
You're such a jealous guy.

But to change,
don't you ever try,
You might be strange,
But you are MY jealous guy :)

Worries me not to be Apart

Woeful tears did I cry,
Explained what you meant to me.
To stop you did I try,
Because without you I just couldn't be.

Did I kill my self respect,
For you who never cared.
To you didn't even effect,
The days of love we shared.

I don't wish to have you back,
And take that all again.
The courage does my heart lack,
To handle the endless pain.

In a tumult is my heart,
Because worries me not to be apart.
What hearts like a dart,
Is for us to part.

The Lane's Story

Even through the shut window pane
The world looked cold
The lonely lonely withered lane
A woeful story told

The wars that were fought
The conflicts that took place
The lessons that were taught
The past does it trace.

Tantalizations of the time
And the tormentations of the age
Tells the lane with a woeful rhyme
Of pity, torture and rage.

Chattered the winds with the lanes
And with the lane, the window panes.

I don't have You

My heart feels no woe,
Nor does it know to smile.
Like the colorless rainbow,
Stretched across a mile.

My mouth knows not to say,
My soul with itself does fight.
I cry every day,
And sob every night.

Feel like diseased with no cure,
Like the mornings with no dew.
Like nothing anymore is pure,
Because I don't have you.

P.S I Love You

What a shame
I couldn't tell you.
I felt the same
Only if you knew

that, P.S I Love You

Well, You'll know some day
How, awake the nights i lay.
Staring at the world above,
Hoping you'll know my love.

Unsaid it was,
Broken by me were the laws.
Fell for you...
Like the morning dew
Because, P.S I Love You

Yeah I lied
And since then I've cried,
I don't like you I said
My heart, almost dead.

You've always meant a lot to me,
Close together, we were meant to be.
Can't live without you.
Only if you knew .
that, P.S I Love You

Wish you knew
what was going on
It was you and only you
I could have sworn

It wasn't easy for me,
Without you to be,
But couldn't tell you
Only if you knew
that, P.S I Love You

P.S I Love You

You Were There

You were there in the morning
And late at night.
Were there when it was gloomy
And when it was bright.

If you search my mind
It's just you that you'll find
You might even dig my heart
If you promise never to part.

Because you were the best
When I needed care
I forgot about the rest
When you were there

When every one was gone
You were with me
Sitting under the trees in the lawn
Was one of the best memory

Of being without you
Was a fear
Everything I could do
For you to be here

You wore a dark gray T-shirt
I wore a dress
You said I was pretty
When I looked like a mess.

You saved me from the guy who was always after me
Couldn't even imagine, without you to be
Time slowed down
When you were around

You said I have got a smile
That takes you to another planet
You said you loved me
Since we had met.

All you said
Was totally fine
Baby, since you were made
You were mine!

I never had to worry
Or take decisions in a hurry
I knew, you would take care
There were no worries when
You were there!!!

Wish You Were Here

Should have at least tried,
To get you along.
Instead I cried,
For what I did was wrong.

Tried to find you in the crowd,
Silent fell the noises loud.
Searched for you in the moon's light,
That luminated oh-so-bright.

Missed you to the core did I,
Into my pillow did I cry.
My heart felt oh so bare,
Because baby, you weren't here.

In your thoughts did my mind dwell,
With tears did my eyes swell.
My soul craved for your presence,
Your glistening aura to add to its essence.

What would end my woes maybe,
Would be having you here, baby.
Close to my heart,
From you, can't I bear to part.

Unity in Diversity

Different creeds,
And different deeds.
Different opinions,
And different dominions.

Different races,
And different places.
Different states,
And different fates.

Each one of us,
Lives in a different frame.
But if we discuss,
We'd know that we're all the same.

All of us can care,
And all of us can feel.
All of us can share,
Or make a mutual deal.

All of us can feel glad,
And cherish the aromatic rain.
All of us can feel sad,
And moan with pain.

Because in a way...
We all stand united.!
And whatever you say,
To know this, you too, are delighted.

So you see...
There is unity,
Wherever there may be.
Existing the diversity!

Love Game

This time I truly wouldn't lie
And tell you how I felt all the pain
Tell you why I said bye
Like I was totally insane.

You paint me a blue sky
And went back to turn in the rain
To keep me happy you try
To have fun and entertain.

I lived in your love game
But you changed the rules everyday
I thought that you were just lame
But you were more than I could say!!!

Maybe it's me
And my blind optimism to blame...
but baby,
At least I did try
To play your love game

Or it was you and your sick need
To give love and take it away
Or it was just in your creed
But the price I had to pay...

You're an expert at saying sorry,
and keeping lives blurry.
But your attitude I just couldn't tame,
I just couldn't play your love game!!!

Tell Me Why

Tell me why,
You didn't care.
You let me cry,
Till my heart went bare.

The days however passed by,
The nights I lay weeping.
My tears as I cry,
Flow to my heart so creeping.

Tell my why,
You just let it be.
Didn't even try ,
Like you didn't love me.

The swears, were all a lie,
The promises nothing but fake.
I wished to die,
My life at stake.

Guess, I'd just let go,
To stop, I wouldn't even try.
And if you ask me so,
I wouldn't even.
Tell you why...

Live Happily Ever After

The Day, the day we said it
After waiting for ages
Our hearts did we knit
Breaking away all the cages.

I blossomed like a flower
You had butterflies in your stomach
My happiness nothing could mar
You thought you had all the luck

At first I tried to undo what I said
I wished further we could wait
But on the path of love, me you led
Because you wanted us to mate

We dwelt among the trodden ways
Besides the springs of dove
Under the sparkling sun rays
In the world of love

We crossed our heart
And hoped to die
If we did ever part
Or for anyone else if we ever sigh

We called each other many a name
The ones as sweet as they could be
Both shared a single aim
Together, always to be

But time wanted us apart
Without each other to be
Broken was my heart
Fine, you just couldn't be.

You respected the decision, however
It was taken for our my good, so
You promised to wait forever
And never to let me go.

We know that we are meant to be
And share forever happiness, joy and laughter
This soon you'd see
And we'd live <u>Happily Ever After!</u>

It Glowed... Like Noting Else

The day was done, and the darkness
Fell from the wings of the night
As a feather is wafted downward
From an Eagle in his flight.

The winds that blew
Recited a rhyme of love
To the birds that flew
In the rainy sky above.

The sun had set,
And the moon set high,
The stars twinkled,
Decorating the sky.

Though it wasn't the day's address,
It glowed... like nothing less.

I Wish

I wish I could,
Kiss away the frowns,
Like you kissed away the fears.
And hold on to your hands,
That wiped away the tears.

The garlanded hands-oh so eloquent.
On my forehead, spoke words of love.
The fingers as elegant,
As in the woods, the alluring dove.

I wish I could,
Just look into,
Your eyes that comfort me.
And provide the same view,
And warmth, that earlier I could see.

I wish I could,
Hold on to you,
Like your snug embraces.
I wish I knew,
That later, of it, Id find no traces.

I wish I could say,
One last time those three magical words,
I and LOVE and YOU.
Before like birds,
To heavens you flew.

Of ignorance,
I pay a huge rate.
Forever would persist the distance,
I WISH it wasn't this late.

Santa Dear!

OH! Santa dear,
Hope you remember.
Us, you've got to cheer,
This beautiful December.

The fog in my eyes,
And the snow on my nose.
Long for a startling surprise,
Wrapped in love and beautiful bows.

The sky with the chill,
And the land that froze,
Long for the thrill,
That Santa must have chose.

On leaves the fresh dew,
And the blossoming flowers too.
Secretly make wishes to you,
Hoping. their hearts, you'd see through.

All of us do pray,
For, you Santa, soon to come.
On your one horse open sleigh,
And end the times so glum.

Come lead by your reindeers,
Aiming to fulfill everyone's wish.
Raining smiles and happy tears,
And making everyone cherish.